DISNEY LEARNING

DISNEY
FROZEN

LET IT GROW

A *FROZEN* GUIDE TO GARDENING

Cynthia Stierle

Reviewed by Catrina T. Adams, PhD,
Botanical Society of America

Lerner Publications • Minneapolis

Lerner Publications Company
A division of Lerner Publishing Group, Inc.
241 First Avenue North
Minneapolis, MN 55401 USA

For reading levels and more information, look up this title at www.lernerbooks.com.

Main body text set in Simoncini Garamond Std.
Typeface provided by Adobe Systems.

Library of Congress Cataloging-in-Publication Data

Names: Stierle, Cynthia, author.
Title: Let it grow : a Frozen guide to gardening / written by Cynthia Stierle ; reviewed by Catrina T. Adams.
Description: Minneapolis, MN : Lerner Publications Company, [2019] | Includes bibliographical references and index.
Identifiers: LCCN 2018020897 (print) | LCCN 2018027528 (ebook) | ISBN 9781541543560 (eb pdf) | ISBN 9781541539136 (lb : alk. paper) | ISBN 9781541546585 (pb : alk. paper)
Subjects: LCSH: Frozen (Motion picture : 2013 : Buck and Lee) | Gardening—Juvenile literature. | Plants—Juvenile literature.
Classification: LCC SB457 (ebook) | LCC SB457 .S82 2019 (print) | DDC 635—dc23

LC record available at https://lccn.loc.gov/2018020897

Manufactured in the United States of America
2-46924-35923-11/14/2018

TABLE OF CONTENTS

LETTER TO EDUCATORS

Dear Educators and Caregivers,

Most children are natural scientists, because science is all about curiosity, hands-on learning, and testing out ideas—exactly what kids do as they learn.

Take the time to look through this book with your students. Most of the activities are demonstrations that show how something works. Encourage your students to ask questions about the activities. What happens if you do something in a different way? As long as you approve, allow your students to test their ideas to see the results.

Throughout, your students will be developing important science-related skills, such as identifying and classifying objects, following directions, and observing and recording data. They will also find out firsthand what plants are and what they need to grow.

Here are a few more tips:

- Always supervise activities and offer to help when needed.
- Encourage your students to be patient. Plants take a long time to grow!
- Science can be messy. Cover your workspace with an old towel or newspaper, and wear clothes that can get dirty.
- Remind your students not to be upset if something doesn't go (or grow!) as planned, because there is always something to learn. Why didn't something work? You can always try the activity again, but do one thing in a different way to see if you get a better result. After all, that's what scientists do!

Most of all, remember to have fun!

5

WHAT DO PLANTS NEED?

Olaf is a magical snowman because he's alive. Did you know that plants are alive too? Though plants can't walk around, they can grow and create new plants. To do that, they need energy from the sun and nutrients from the soil, air, and water. What happens if a plant doesn't get enough of those things? Try this activity to find out.

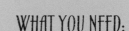

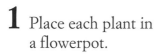

WHAT YOU NEED:

- 4 small flowerpots
- 4 of the same type of small plant seedlings, all about the same size (you can use the bean seedlings from another experiment; see pages 20–21)
- 4 craft sticks and tape
- Garden signs

1 Place each plant in a flowerpot.

2 Create garden signs for each pot that say the following:
- Plant 1: Water and Sunlight
- Plant 2: Sunlight and No Water
- Plant 3: Water and No Sunlight
- Plant 4: No Water and No Sunlight

3 Cut out the garden signs. Tape a craft stick to each garden sign, and insert one stick into each pot.

4 Follow the steps on each garden sign, and compare the plants every week. What changes do you notice in each pot?

WHAT DO YOU THINK?

Why do some plants grow well in the sun but not in the shade? What would happen if a plant was watered with salt water instead of fresh water?

PRETTY PLANTS

Olaf has feet for walking, eyes for seeing, and a mouth for talking. Each part of a plant does something special for that plant. Explore and learn about the parts of a typical plant by going on a scavenger hunt.

ACTIVITY
Plant Scavenger Hunt

1 Look at the plant diagram, and think about the different parts of plants.

2 In your notebook, create a checklist of plant parts to look for on your scavenger hunt. Write down items such as flowers, seeds, and roots. Use the plant diagram for help!

3 With an adult, walk through your yard, a park, or even a garden center. Look for and check off the plant parts described on your list.

WHAT YOU NEED:

- Notebook
- A pen or pencil

Leaves make food for the plant by using sunlight, air, and water.

Fruits protect and scatter the seeds.

Flowers attract pollinators.

Stems support the plant and move water and nutrients through it.

Seeds grow into new plants.

Roots hold a plant in the ground and take up water and minerals from the soil.

NOTE: *You can also take pictures of the plant parts, print them out, and use them in the next activity!*

ACTIVITY
Create a Plant Picture

1 Sort the pictures. How many different leaves, stems, flowers, seeds, and roots are there?

2 Select some of the pictures to arrange and glue onto the heavy paper to make your own plant.

3 Name your plant! Write labels for the plant parts.

WHAT YOU NEED:

- Plant pictures from magazines, newspapers, or the Internet
- Heavy paper or poster board
- Glue stick
- Marker

WHAT DO YOU THINK?

What other words can you think of to describe the plant parts? How are the leaves alike? How are they different? What time of year is it? How would the plants look at a different time of year?

SNACK TIME FOR SVEN

Sven is always trying to eat Olaf's nose. Who can blame him? Carrots are yummy! Did you know that the orange part of the carrot is a root? Many plants have parts that are good to eat. Some plant parts are also good for making prints!

PLANT PARTS YOU COULD USE:

ROOTS & TUBERS
Potatoes, Sweet Potatoes, Carrots

STEMS & STALKS
Celery, Asparagus

FLOWER BUDS
Broccoli

LEAVES
Romaine Lettuce, Cabbage, Spinach, Brussels Sprouts

SEEDS & FRUITS
Corn on the Cob, String Beans, Apples, Pears

ACTIVITY
Plant Prints

WHAT YOU NEED:

- One of each plant part (suggestions listed on opposite page)
- Knife
- Paper towels
- Paintbrush
- Washable tempera paint (one or more colors)
- Plastic plates (one for each color)
- Heavy paper or poster board

1 With an adult's help, cut large fruits or vegetables in half, blotting on a paper towel to dry.

2 Brush a thin layer of paint onto the plates. Dip the flat surface of the plant into the paint. Then press it onto the heavy paper to make a print.

3 Repeat the stamping with other plant parts and other colors to make a picture.

WHAT DO YOU THINK?

What other plant parts do you think Sven might like to eat? Which plant parts do you like to eat?

PUTTING DOWN ROOTS

Most plants have roots that go into the soil, where they take up water and minerals to stay alive. While a carrot's orange root grows down into the ground, its green stems and leaves grow up toward the sky. Try growing things up and down with these activities.

ACTIVITY
Growing Up

WHAT YOU NEED:
- Carrot with top (greens) still attached, rinsed
- Knife
- Shallow dish
- Water

1 With an adult's help, trim both ends of the carrot, leaving about 1 inch (2.5 cm) of greens and 1 inch of carrot root.

2 Set the carrot cut side down into the dish, and place it in a bright window. Add water to cover about half of the remaining carrot root.

3 Check on the carrot every day, adding water if needed. The carrot tops should begin to regrow within a week.

NOTE: *Try this experiment with more than one carrot top at a time if you want to compare and contrast the results.*

ACTIVITY
Growing Down

WHAT YOU NEED:

- Avocado
- Knife
- 3 or 4 toothpicks
- Clear glass or jar
- Water

1 Ask an adult to cut open the avocado and remove and rinse the seed. Hold the seed so the narrow end points up. Carefully insert toothpicks around the middle of the seed, spacing them evenly.

2 Lower the avocado seed into the glass so that the toothpicks rest on the rim. Fill the glass so that half of the seed is covered with water.

3 Change the water every few days. In about two weeks the seed's outer layer will start falling off, and the seed will begin to split open. A few weeks later, a root should begin growing down out of the seed.

WHAT DO YOU THINK?

Why do we eat some parts of the plant and not others? What other plants can be grown from roots or tubers? What about potatoes or beets?

MOVING AROUND

Kristoff moves heavy blocks of ice through the snow. Stems and stalks keep things moving too. They send water and food to different parts of the plant. To see where the water goes, try this activity using celery stalks.

ACTIVITY
Fantasy Forest

WHAT YOU NEED:

- Tall, clear glass
- Water
- Red or blue food coloring (20 drops or more)
- Knife
- Celery stalk with leaves (the inner, lighter stalks work best)

1 Fill a tall, clear glass half full with water. Add food coloring and mix well. With an adult's help, cut 1 inch (2.5 cm) off the bottom of the celery stalk. Place the celery stalk in the glass.

2 Check on the celery stalk every few hours. Do you see the colored water moving into the stalk or the leaves?

3 When the leaves have changed color, remove the celery from the water. Cut off the bottom and look at it.

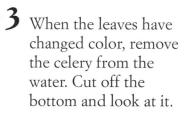

Before

After

WHAT DO YOU THINK?

What part of the stalk transports the water? What would happen if the celery was put into salt water instead of fresh water? What would happen if lettuce was used instead of celery?

COLORFUL MAGIC

It's amazing to see a garden filled with colorful flowers that attract insects and birds. It's also amazing to watch Elsa do her magic. Did you ever wish you could do magic? In this transformation activity, you can change white flowers into colorful, bright flowers that look magical!

ACTIVITY
Arendelle Bouquet

WHAT YOU NEED:

- 4 glass containers
- Warm water
- Red, green, yellow, and blue food coloring (20 drops or more each)
- 12 to 20 white carnations
- Scissors
- Small vase

1 Fill each glass halfway with warm water and one of the food coloring colors and mix well.

2 With an adult's help, trim 1 inch (2.5 cm) from the bottom of each flower stem. Divide the flowers among the containers.

3 Observe the flowers every few hours. If a flower's color doesn't change, trim the stem again. Leave the flowers overnight.

4 The next day, remove the flowers from the glasses. Trim the stems again, and place them in a vase filled with clear water. Enjoy the magical colors in the bouquet!

WHAT DO YOU THINK?

 Which color moves the fastest through the stems to the flower and leaves? Which color moves the slowest?

LEAVES OF SUMMER

Leaves make food—and get that green color—with help from a substance called chlorophyll. Did you know other colors can be hidden in those green leaves? You might see the other colors in autumn, when days get shorter and colder. But you can get a sneak peek in summer or spring.

ACTIVITY
Hidden Colors

WHAT YOU NEED:

- Small glass
- White coffee filter cut into two strips 1 inch (2.5 cm) wide and slightly longer than the glass
- Pencil and tape
- 3 to 5 green leaves from the same tree
- Resealable plastic bag and rolling pin
- Isopropyl (rubbing) alcohol
- Plastic fork

1 Roll one end of each coffee filter strip around the pencil. Rest the pencil on the rim of the glass. Adjust the strips so that they almost touch the bottom of the glass. Then tape them to the pencil and remove.

2 Tear up the leaves, place in the plastic bag, and seal. Mash the leaves with the rolling pin.

3 Place the leaves in the glass, and pour in rubbing alcohol to just cover them. Mash a bit more with the fork. (The liquid should turn green.)

4 Insert the strips, which should just touch the liquid, letting the pencil rest on the rim. After 60 to 90 minutes, remove the strips and let them dry. You should be able to see bands of color!

WHAT DO YOU THINK?

Are the bands on the strips different or the same? What would happen if you used different kinds of leaves? What colors might you see? What would happen if you used leaves that had already changed color?

OUT OF THE WINDOW

Anna opens a castle window to see the big yellow sunflowers growing outside. Like many plants, sunflowers grow from seeds. Inside each little seed is a baby plant waiting for just the right conditions to sprout into a new plant. You can look out a window too and see seeds sprout before your eyes.

WHAT YOU NEED:

- 5 to 7 cotton balls
- Spray bottle filled with water
- Clear resealable plastic sandwich bag
- 4 or 5 dry (not canned) beans
- Tape
- 2 or 3 small cups filled with soil
- Wooden stick or dowel

ACTIVITY
Sprouting Seeds

1 Spray the cotton balls to wet them, and place them in the bag. They should be damp but not dripping.

20

2 Place 4 or 5 dry beans in the bag on top of the cotton balls. Seal the bag, leaving a slight opening for airflow.

3 Tape the bag to a warm, sunny window.

4 The beans should begin to sprout in 3 to 5 days. Moisten the cotton balls if they are drying out. Open the bag more if the seedlings need room to grow.

5 When there are two or three leaves on the seedlings, plant each in a small cup of soil.

6 Insert a stick or dowel into the soil next to one of the plants, as shown. Watch the bean plant grow up and around the stick!

WHAT DO YOU THINK?

How many of the beans sprouted? What would happen if you used different kinds of beans?

SCATTERING SEEDS

Olaf loves blowing dandelion seeds into the breeze.
He probably doesn't know that he's helping the dandelion
create new dandelions, just by scattering its seeds. What seeds
can be scattered by someone walking around?
Slip on an old pair of socks to see.

WHAT YOU NEED:

- Old, worn pair of adult woolly cotton socks (should fit easily over your shoes)
- A safe area that is overgrown with seed-bearing weeds
- Potting soil and plastic spoon
- Small baking pan and rectangular block
- Spray bottle filled with water

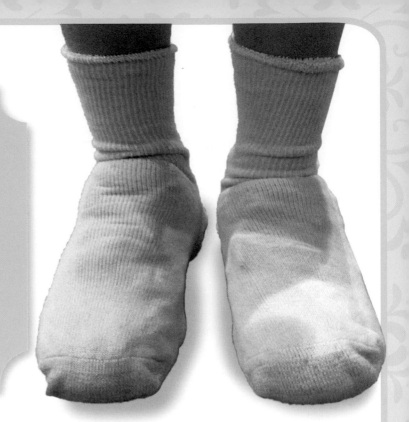

ACTIVITY
Sock Seeds

1 Pull the pair of socks on over your shoes. Walk in a safe area where seeds might be found. After the walk, remove the socks.

2 Use the spoon to fill the socks with soil. Place filled socks with the bottoms facing up in the baking pan, and spray with water.

3 Place the pan in a warm, bright place. Put the block under one end of the baking pan. Add water to the pan so that the ends of the socks touch the water but aren't soaked.

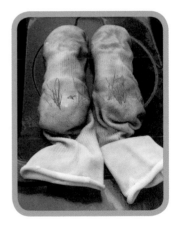

4 Add water to the pan as it dries, and mist the socks to keep them moist. After about 10 to 14 days, see if anything grows up from the sock.

NOTE: *Always check yourself for ticks after walking in any tall grass.*

WHAT DO YOU THINK?

What makes the seeds you collected cling to socks? What time of year is it now? Are there lots of seeds out at this time or not many? If anything sprouted from your socks, what kinds of plants could they be?

A BRAND-NEW WORLD

Anna and Elsa's friends the trolls live in the mountains where they have everything they need to survive. A terrarium is a closed, see-through container that contains everything a plant needs to stay alive, including water. Here's how to create your own little plant world.

WHAT YOU NEED:

- Clear 2-liter plastic bottle with cap, cleaned and label removed
- Marker, scissors, and clear tape
- Pea-size gravel (like aquarium gravel)
- Potting soil
- Small plant
- Spray bottle filled with water
- Small stones, twigs, bark pieces, or other items for decoration

ACTIVITY
Troll Terrarium

1 Draw a line around the bottle, about 5 inches (13 cm) up the side. With an adult's help, cut the bottle into two pieces. Use tape to cover any sharp edges.

3 Place the seedling on top of the soil, making sure the leaves don't touch the sides of the bottle. Add soil around the plant's base until level. Gently tamp the soil down. Then mist the leaves and soil with water.

2 Fill the bottom of the bottle with 1 inch (2.5 cm) of gravel. Add 1 inch of soil on top of the gravel.

4 Decorate the terrarium with your favorite *Frozen* characters and other items. Cut two 0.5-inch (1.3 cm) slits on opposite sides of the bottom half of the bottle. Gently squeeze the bottom to slip the top of the bottle over it. Screw the cap onto the bottle.

5 Set the bottle in a place with bright, indirect light. Eventually, drops of water should form on the inside of the bottle. If too much water collects, remove the cap and let the terrarium dry out.

6 If drops of water are not forming on the inside, open the cap and add water to the terrarium. The plant will grow with the right amount of water in the terrarium.

WHAT DO YOU THINK?

Why do some plants grow better in terrariums than others? What happens if you make two terrariums, each with a different plant? Which do you think will grow better?

PUTTING IT ALL TOGETHER

The trolls gave young Kristoff the tender care he needed to grow. Now that you know what plants need to grow, you can give a young plant a little tender care to make it grow. Here's how to grow a grassy troll.

ACTIVITY
Grow a Grassy Troll

WHAT YOU NEED:

- 8-inch-long (20.3 cm) nylon stocking, foot portion included
- Scissors
- Empty yogurt cup or small pot (without a hole in the base)
- 2 tablespoons of grass seed
- 1 cup of soil
- 1 small rubber band
- Water

1 Cut and stretch the stocking over the cup. Push the toe of the stocking down into the cup so that you can add seed and soil. Put the grass seed into the stocking foot, and then fill it with soil almost to the top.

2 Remove the stocking from the cup, and tie a knot at the top so that the soil is tightly packed. Leave a couple of inches of stocking behind the knot.

3 To form a nose, pinch a bit of soil and stocking and shape into a small ball. Then twist the ball and secure it with a rubber band.

4 Fill the cup about halfway with lukewarm water. Briefly run the stocking head under a faucet to soak it. Then place the head in the cup with the extra stocking tail hanging down into the water. The grass seed should be on top.

5 Put the troll in a sunny window, and keep it watered but not too wet. In a few days, sprouts should be visible. In about a week, the troll will have some hair.

6 Once the troll has a full head of hair, decorate the face and cup with eyes, clothes, and feet for your grassy troll.

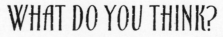

WHAT DO YOU THINK?

How does your troll change every day? What would happen if you did not water your troll? What would happen if you placed it in a shady place? How does the water reach the grassy head?

KEEP GROWING!

Olaf is so happy to experience summer with his friends—he loves seeing all the things that grow. There are many more things to discover about plants in the mountains of Arendelle—and in your own neighborhood. Keep asking questions to learn more about growing things.

THINGS TO THINK ABOUT WHEN MAKING OBSERVATIONS:

Look very closely at what you are observing. Sometimes changes are very small and not easy to see.

What words can you think of to describe a plant or part of a plant? Is it fluffy or fuzzy? Smooth or prickly? Thin or fat? Bumpy or wet? What color is it? How big or small is it?

Look at the things around the plant that might change the way it grows. Is it sunny? Is it shady? Is the air hot? Is it cold?

GLOSSARY

bud: a small knob on a plant that grows into a leaf or flower

chlorophyll: the green material in a plant that uses light to create food for the plant

diagram: a drawing, sketch, plan, or chart that helps explain something

energy: the ability of something to do work

mineral: a solid material in the earth that does not come from an animal or plant

nutrient: a material such as a protein, mineral, or vitamin that people, animals, and plants need to stay strong and healthy

seedling: a young plant that grew from a seed

sprout: to begin to grow and produce buds

stalk: the main stem of a plant from which the leaves and flowers grow

terrarium: a glass or plastic container for growing small plants or raising small land animals

tuber: the thick underground stem of a plant such as a potato

TO LEARN MORE

Books

Brown, Renata Fossen. *Gardening Lab for Kids*. Beverly, MA: Quarry Books, 2014.
Read this book to find more gardening experiments that help you make, grow, and harvest your own garden.

Cornell, Kari. *The Nitty-Gritty Gardening Book: Fun Projects for All Seasons*. Minneapolis: Millbrook Press, 2015.
Check out this book for fun gardening projects and activities.

Dichter, Paul. *The Night Sky: A* Frozen *Discovery Book*. Minneapolis: Lerner Publications, 2019.
Learn more about nature and the night sky with the help of your favorite *Frozen* characters in this book.

Websites

My First Garden
https://extension.illinois.edu/firstgarden/
Visit this website to learn more about how to plan and start growing your own garden.

Photosynthesis: How Plants Make Food and Energy
http://easyscienceforkids.com/all-about-photosynthesis/
What causes plants to grow? How do they eat? Check out this website to learn!

Stone Trolls Craft
http://cdnvideo.dolimg.com/cdn_assets
/300e8e9929fa9ae36807a5d82fc5a838bb411ef0.pdf
Follow the steps of this outdoor craft project to create your own stone trolls from *Frozen*. Use them to decorate your garden!

INDEX

Photographs and Illustrations